ODD**TIME**DRUM
GROOVEMASTERY

The Complete Guide to Making Any Odd Time Signature Easy to Play on Drums

BUSTER**BIRCH**

FUNDAMENTAL**CHANGES**

Odd Time Drum Groove Mastery

The Complete Guide to Making Any Odd Time Signature Easy to Play on Drums

ISBN: 978-1-78933-436-4

Published by www.fundamental-changes.com

www.fundamental-changes.com

@fundamentalchanges

Join our free Facebook Community of Cool Musicians

www.facebook.com/groups/fundamentalguitar

For over 350 free guitar lessons with Videos, check out

www.fundamental-changes.com

Cover Image: Shutterstock, Africa Studio

Musicians:

All audio tracks written and produced by Buster Birch

Contents

About the Author

Buster Birch is an award-winning jazz musician and educator from London, UK. He was a professorial member of the jazz faculty at Trinity Laban Conservatoire of music for seven years, where he taught improvisation, musicianship, jazz repertoire and jazz history classes. He has also lectured at The Royal Academy of Music, The Guildhall School of Music & Drama and Middlesex University.

Buster is a busy freelance jazz drummer who has worked with a great many of the UK's finest jazz musicians. He has an honours degree in music from the University of London and a post-graduate diploma in jazz performance from the Guildhall School of Music and Drama. He also studied at the Drummers Collective in New York City and privately with Jim Chapin and Joe Morello (of The Dave Brubeck Quartet).

He has performed at virtually every concert hall and jazz club in London, as well as major international festivals; he has toured in over thirty countries and recorded nearly forty albums. He has been a member of three world music groups with whom he recorded and toured extensively, and has played for world-class orchestras including The Royal Philharmonic Orchestra, and deputised on West End shows.

He is director of The Original UK Jazz Summer School, the UK's longest running jazz summer school and winner of the Parliamentary Award for Jazz Education. The summer school is a week-long residential course for singers and all instrumentalists of all ages and experience levels.

He is co-founder and leader of BYMT Jazz School which runs weekly jazz improvisation classes for school children at the county music centre. In 2017, BYMT Jazz School won the prestigious Will Michael Diploma Award for Jazz Education – a national award recognising "outstanding commitment to jazz education" and "acknowledging the work of those field practitioners who are actually delivering jazz education and, in many cases, helping to combat the widespread jazz phobia among classroom music teachers and instrumental tutors."

He created his own critically acclaimed show **www.busterplaysbuster.com** which features the Buster Birch Jazz Quartet playing live and in sync to the screening of classic Buster Keaton silent movies, for which he arranged and scored over 4hrs of music. In 2023 Buster plays Buster won the Audience Award at The Chichester International Film Festival – a major UK film festival featuring 110 screenings over 22 days.

Buster is a member of the following bands: ARQ (The Alison Rayner Quintet) – winners of the Parliamentary Award for "Best UK Jazz Ensemble" and the British Jazz Award public vote for "Best Small Group". He is also a member of The Jo Fooks Quartet, Heads South, The London Jazz Trio and The Halstead Jazz Club Big Band.

He has lots of great content, video lessons and free resources for drummers available on his website **www. busterbirch.co.uk**

Introduction

I will always remember an uncomfortable situation that occurred early in my career and taught me an important lesson about playing in odd time signatures. As a music student I had spent a fair amount of time practising odd time beats from a famous drum book, so I felt pretty confident when I received a call from a great Balkan jazz guitarist. He said I had been recommended for his trio and asked if I could play in seven. "Sure, sounds like fun." I replied.

He wrote original tunes based on old Balkan folk music, mostly in 7/8, and sent me the audio tracks a couple of days before the gig. When I listened to them, I soon realised that everything I had practiced before was of no use to me! All the groups of seven I had learned from the book were arranged in divisions of 2-2-3, but this music was all based around dividing the bar into 3-2-2! (Don't worry if this makes no sense right now, it will later!)

These new rhythmic phrases felt very awkward to me, and I had to count like mad when I first practiced with his recordings. Fortunately, I had a couple of days to shed everything, managed to get through the gig OK, and he asked me to join his trio. Over the next 10 years we played all over the UK and recorded a couple of albums. I got very comfortable with 7/8 in a 3-2-2 clave and it made me appreciate how versatile odd time signatures can be.

To play any odd time music well, you must be completely aware of what is happening around you. You must understand what the other musicians are doing and how their parts groove together, because only then can you really play *with* them. This doesn't just mean the general time signature, but also how each bar is subdivided and the melodic shape of the line or riff. The key is to first analyse what is happening musically and only then think about what to play on the drums, not just your favourite odd time beat. I call this *reverse-engineered* drumming.

I've used this reverse-engineered approach to structure this book, so instead of just learning a bunch of odd time grooves you will start by listening to the included play-along tracks in different time signatures. Once you understand the structure of the riff you will use fundamental ingredients to sculpt these basic beats and create sophisticated grooves that complement the music. By doing this, you will learn to create your own grooves in *any* odd time signature. Focusing on the rhythmic shape of the riff will help you *feel* the odd time groove and help you avoid the pain I experienced with those first Balkan folk tunes!

In this book I will refer to musical terms like *duple meter*, *triple meter* and *pulse*, so if you are not absolutely clear on their meaning, please check out the "Clarification of Musical Terms and Definitions" section in the appendix.

Also, it's important to check out the recommended listening playlist on Spotify, as I refer to it throughout the book.

https://geni.us/otspotify

Get the Audio

The audio files for this book are available to download for free from **www.fundamental-changes.com.** The link is in the top right-hand corner of the webpage. Simply select this book title from the drop-down menu and follow the instructions to get the audio.

We recommend that you download the files directly to your computer, not to your tablet, and extract them there before adding them to your media library. On the download page there is a help PDF and we also provide technical support via the contact form.

www.fundamental-changes.com

Instagram: **FundamentalChanges**

Chapter One – Odd Time Clave

It's all just twos and threes!

Any odd time signature can be subdivided into groups of 2s and 3s.

If the time signature has a /4 underneath (for example 5/4 or 7/4), then these 2- and 3-note groupings apply to the 1/4 notes.

If the time signature has an /8 underneath (for example 5/8, 7/8 or 9/8), then the 2- and 3-note groupings apply to the 1/8th notes.

The way the 2s and 3s are grouped in each bar creates the rhythmic *shape* of the music. Or, as I like to call it, the *odd time clave* (pronounced *kla-vey*).

In a bar of 5/4 time signature, the pulse can be grouped into 3+2 or 2+3. So, the first thing you have to figure out is which way around the odd time clave is being played. To do this, listen to:

- Any placements of a chord change within the bar
- The rhythmic *shape* of the bassline, guitar riff, or musical phrase

Let's get started.

Listen to the famous piano intro to Take 5 (using the QR code below to open the Spotify playlist, or just type the link in your browser).

https://geni.us/otspotify

We know it is played in 5/4 time, but if you pay attention to the chords and melody you can hear that the riff is divided into 3+2 by the rhythmic shape of the melody and the chord change on beat 4. So, instead of counting it "12345" it feels more natural to count **123,12** and hear the music as 3+2.

Now you are thinking in an odd time clave!

Now you understand how the 5/4 groove is divided and what the other musicians are playing, you can begin to play a suitable beat. Your choices are narrowed by the musical division of the bar and your groove will feel more natural because you are fitting it to the rhythmic shape of the music. We will take this a step further later and match the pitch of the drums to the riff, but understanding the phrasing of the odd time clave is the first essential step to locking in with the music.

The Melody of The Groove

When you focus on the melody of the piece you will find the drum groove much easier to play and remember. In fact, it is a natural extension of the twos and threes approach. A good starting point is to sing the groove because having it strongly in your in your head helps to lock your coordination and note choice to the melody to articulate the tune on the drum set.

This is where pitch and orchestration come in to play.

Often, we tend to use snare and bass drum, which means we only have two pitches to think about. However, we can use the toms, hi-hat lifts and other sounds to create more pitch options that closely mirror the music.

The idea is to try and match the melody of your groove to the melody of the tune, riff, or bassline you are supporting. I'm not just talking about rhythm, I mean pitch as well. This requires careful listening to the other instruments and applying their melodic phrasing to the drum kit.

To begin, try to pick out and highlight significant points in the melodic line using different sounds on the drum kit. The bass, guitar and keyboard are a good place to start, but your melodic phrasing can also come from the horns or singers.

Start by identifying the high and low pitches of the music and play them on the bass and snare drum. You don't have to play every note, just pick out the more significant ones and notice where they sit in the bar.

Ask yourself how other lines, such as horn parts or backing vocals, fit with the bass or guitar riff. Is there is a question-and-answer structure you can highlight? Does the harmonic sequence fit over a number of bars? If so, where is the loop point? Are there two chords in a bar? On which beat do they do they change?

The idea is to condense everything you're hearing into a single melody line that can be sung then orchestrated using the available sounds on the kit to closely mirror the musical phrase, and to play it with a relaxed feel that locks everyone together.

A couple of drummers come to mind as complete masters of this technique, such as David Garibaldi with Tower of Power, and Dave Weckl with The GRP Big Band. Check out their tracks in the Spotify playlist.

Of course, there are some circumstances (like soloing over a vamp) where you can take the opposite approach and play right across the melodic phrase with a contradictory beat, but that's a skill for much later down the line. Let's learn to lock in first!

Chapter Two – 1/4-Note Odd Time Primer

Let's quickly learn the basic "three and two" building blocks of 1/4 note odd time signatures. 1/4 note signatures use *duple* meter, which means each beat is divided into two even subdivisions. In other words, we count "one *and* two *and* three *and…*" etc.

Bear with me as we are going to start very simply with basic 1/4 note beats, then sculpt these ideas into more sophisticated grooves later.

Remember, when playing odd times everything comes down to strong rhythmic groups of two and three 1/4 notes.

These can be organised in four ways depending on the number of beats in each group, and the note on which the pattern starts.

Groups of Two

These can be organised as:

- Two quarter notes starting on the *bass* drum

Or,

- Two quarter notes starting on the *snare* drum.

Play each one a few times until you can comfortably feel the shape of the rhythm as you count **1**+2+**1**+2+

Two 1/4 Notes Starting on The Bass Drum

Example 2a

Two 1/4 Notes Starting on The Snare Drum

Example 2b

Groups of Three

These can be organised as:

- Three quarter notes starting on the *bass* drum

Or,

- Three quarter notes starting on the *snare* drum

Play each one a few times until you can comfortably feel the shape of the rhythm as you count **1+2+3+1+2+3+**

Three 1/4 Notes Starting on The Bass Drum

Example 2c

Example 2d

Example 2e

Three 1/4 Notes Starting on The Snare Drum

Example 2f

Example 2g

Example 2h

At first, it can feel strange playing a snare hit at the beginning of the bar. It's probably something you are not used to doing, but it's a very important skill in odd time playing and will open up many more musical possibilities with odd time phrasing.

Chapter Three – 5/4

3+2 Odd Time Clave with 1/8th Note Placements

Listen to audio track A, which is a simple riff in 5/4. There is a chord change on the fourth beat of the bar which suggests that the odd time clave is 3+2.

Count "**1**+2+3+**1**+2+" and hear how well that fits with the music. Now count "**1**+2+**1**+2+3+" and hear how "lumpy" that feels.

Next, listen to the bassline and notice how the lowest notes are played on the first and fourth beat in the bar. That is a good place for the bass drum and we can fit the snare around that.

Let's combine the fundamental ingredients from Example 2c (a group of three) and Example 2a (a group of two) to create the basic three-two division of this groove.

Example 3a

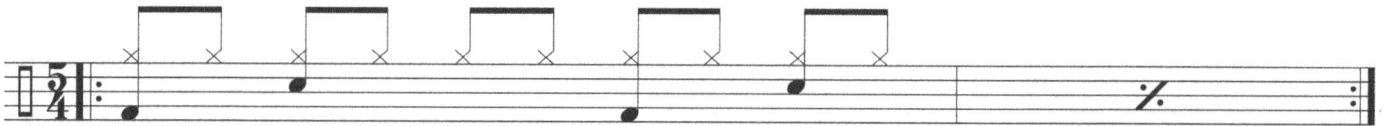

Now we have the basic shape, let's start sculpting the groove to add more interest. A hi-hat lift draws attention to the note that follows as it shuts, so adding a hi-hat lift at the end of the bar helps to emphasize the down beat of the next bar. Playing a snare drum on the third upbeat adds a little funkiness.

Example 3b

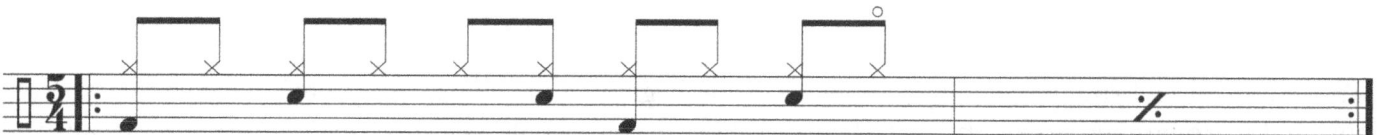

The next variation uses a hi-hat lift on the "and" of beat 3 to emphasize the down beat on beat 4, and adds an extra bass hit to the end of the bar.

Example 3c

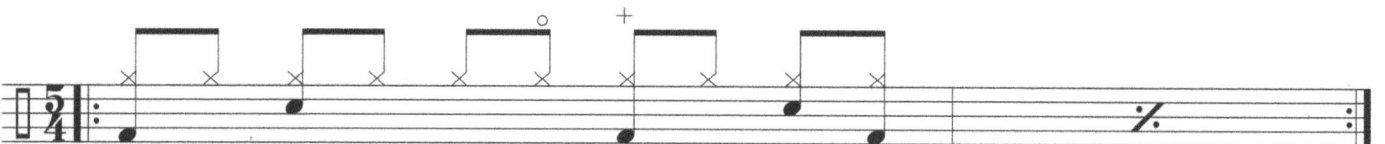

This last variation adds some bass drum to help mirror the shape of the riff.

Example 3d

These variations all feature simple embellishments that don't change the fundamental shape of the groove and are useful decorations you should become comfortable with.

Now try mixing the previous examples as you play along to the track. Try to sit nicely in the groove and keep your execution clean.

As your skills develop, you will learn to rely on your own taste and judgement to decide how busy to make the groove. Whether you choose to closely mirror the riff, or simply outline the basic shape is up to you, and there's a sliding scale you can adjust as you play until you get the right balance for the track. However, before this can happen you must work through many variations to develop the coordination and language required to make these musical adjustments in real time.

2+3 Odd Time Clave with 1/8th Note Placements

Listen to track B, a simple riff in 5/4. Count "**1**+2+**1**+2+3+" and hear how that clave fits with the music.

Each chord lasts for a whole bar and the sequence repeats every four bars. As there is no chord change in the middle of the bar, listen to the bass riff to hear the odd time clave of 2+3 clearly.

Combining the basic ingredients of examples 2a and 2e creates the shape of this groove.

Example 3e

Add an extra bass hit to mirror the bassline and a hi-hat lift to emphasise the one.

Example 3f

Now experiment with your own 2+3 variations as you play along with the track.

Combining 3+2 and 2+3 Odd Time Clave with 1/8th Note Placements

The grooves so far have all been a repeating one bar phrase. However, it is possible to vary the clave patterns to create longer phrases over a number of bars. This next example features a four-bar phrase with the clave pattern switched around on the last bar.

Listen to track C and count | 1+2+3+1+2+ | 1+2+3+1+2+ | 1+2+3+1+2+ | 1+2+1+2+3+ |

The clave switch in the final bar has a profound effect on the phrase. Just as you get used to the 3+2 feel, it flips around and throws off the count to create tension and displace the expectation of beat one in the next four bars.

It's all in 5/4, but mixing different 2 and 3 clave patterns is a great way to create interesting odd-time riffs.

Here are the four bars created using basic 1/8th note ingredients.

Example 3g

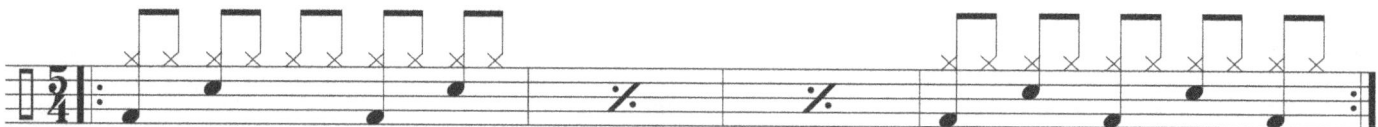

Let's add some simple embellishments to the pattern.

Example 3h

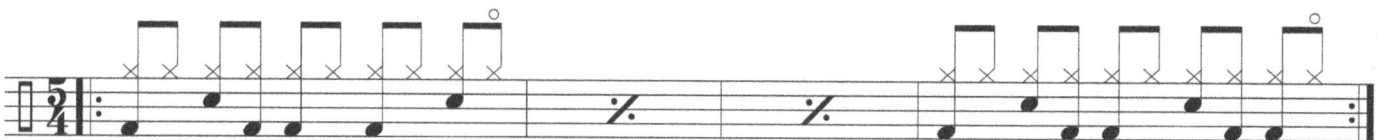

You will probably find that playing this beat on its own isn't too difficult, but when you play along with the audio track it is more challenging. This is because your brain is trying to process how the beat connects with the music, and the melody and harmony shifting around can really throw you. It's exactly what I talked about in the intro when I got my introduction to Balkan folk music!

It's essential to get comfortable with the phrasing within the music *before* you play, to feel the groove and subdivide the bar accordingly. It's never a case of just counting the time signature and treating an odd time as a mathematical exercise.

That's why it's absolutely vital to practice along with the audio tracks, not just practice the beats on their own.

OK, now it's time to add some 1/16th notes and get funky!

3+2 Odd Time Clave with 1/16th Note Placements

Adding 1/16th notes to the groove opens up many variation opportunities to the basic subdivisions.

Listen to track D and count along "1e&a 2e&a 3e&a 1e&a 2e&a".

This groove is a 3+2 clave and the chords form a two-bar sequence. The slight variations in the beat help to establish the two-bar phrase.

The basic ingredients are again 2c and 2a, but notice the 1/16th note *push* on beat two of the audio track. The keyboard and bass anticipate the chord by a 1/16th note, so let's push the snare to match it.

Example 3i

The riff also features a syncopated 1/16th note rhythm at the end of the phrase. Use the snare and bass drum to mirror it.

Example 3j

Now experiment with your own variations.

2+3 Odd Time Clave with 1/16th Note Placements

Listen to track E and count "**1**+2+**1**+2+3+". The clave is 2+3 and the riff uses a two-bar combination of 1/8th note fundamentals.

Start by playing the basic beats to get the shape of the groove. Flipping around the snare and bass drum in bar two displaces beat one and helps to establish the two-bar phrase.

Example 3k

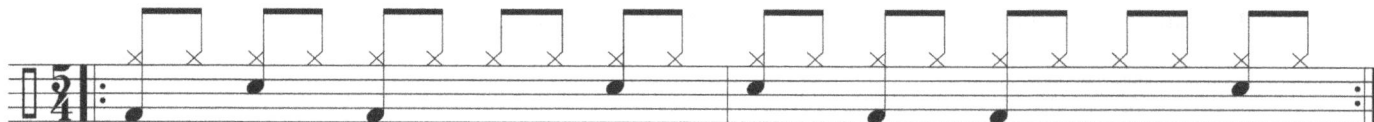

Now add these 1/16th notes and embellishments to mirror the melody of the groove more closely.

Example 3l

Once again, experiment with your own variations as you play along with the track.

Combining 2+3 and 3+2 Odd Time Clave with 1/16th Note Placements

This next example is a four-bar phrase with the clave pattern switched around in the second and fourth bars.

Listen to track F and count "| **1**+2+**1**+2+3+ | **1**+2+3+**1**+2+ |" The chord sequence follows a four-bar pattern but the drum groove works with this two-bar sequence.

Start by playing the basic 1/8th note groove and then repeat for the next two bars.

Example 3m

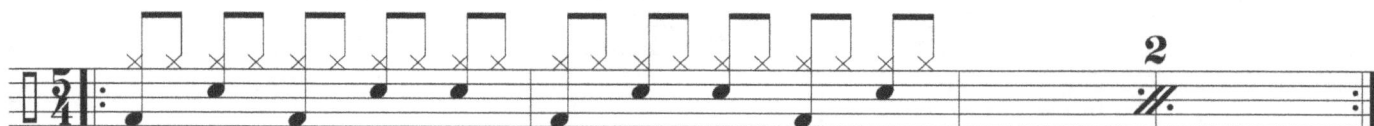

Now move some of the bass and snare hits to these 1/16th placements and add hi-hat lifts to more closely mirror the melody of the groove.

Example 3n

Now we are creating some very interesting phrasing in 5/4. While these can be challenging to hear at first, you just need to learn to hear everything as 2s and 3s and it'll all start to fall into place.

Start by figuring out the odd time clave, then listen to the melodic shape of the riff. Once you can hear that, the groove will quickly make sense. Remember, once you've learned the groove, never just practice it on its own! Play along with the music so your brain can learn to connect what you are playing with the other instruments.

The trick is to always experiment with your own variations while playing along to the same tracks. Just as you learned to play in 4/4, learning to play in 5/4 is simply a case of learning the basic subdivisions and spending time playing them.

Chapter Four – 7/4

We will now apply the same thinking to 7/4. Mathematically speaking, 7/4 is just another two beats added to 5/4 but now there are a few more options of where to place the extra two-beat subdivisions.

2+2+3 Odd Time Clave

Listen to track G and count along "**1**+2+**1**+2+**1**+2+3+" until you feel comfortable with the 2+2+3 clave of this riff, then use the following basic 1/8th note divisions to create the basic shape of the groove.

Example 4a

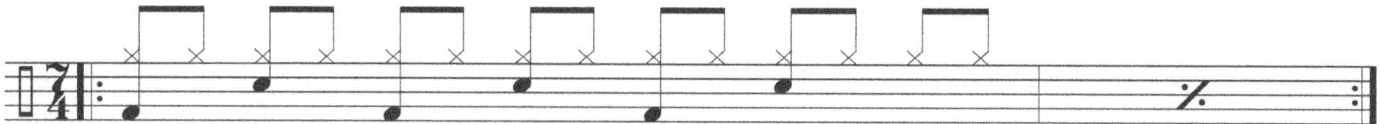

Next add some 1/8th notes on the bass drum and a hi-hat lift to closely match the melody of the groove.

Example 4b

This variation has a busier bass drum and some 1/16th notes to make everything a bit funkier.

Example 4c

3+2+2 Odd Time Clave

Listen to track H and count "1+2+3+1+2+1+2+" along with the music. This can feel a little strange if you are not used to counting seven in this way. Make sure you can hear the shape of the riff and get comfortable counting 3+2+2. Take your time and listen to the track several times before you play along.

Start with simple 1/8th note ingredients to get the basic shape of the groove.

Example 4d

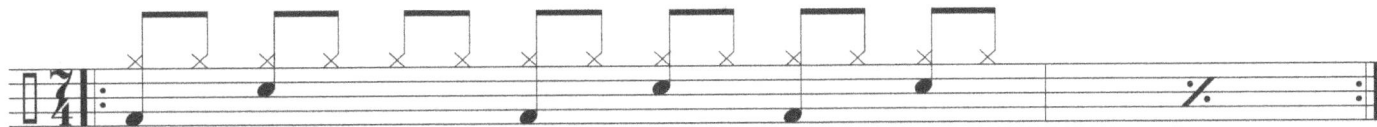

Now adjust the second and seventh beat to match the rhythm of the bass riff.

Example 4e

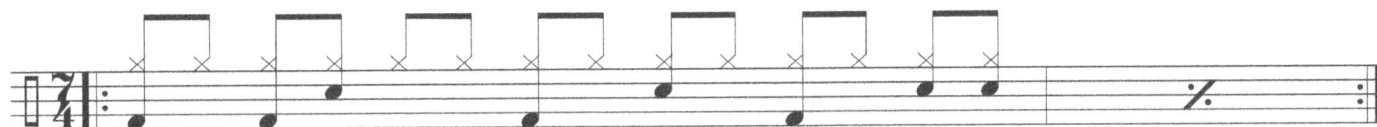

The next variation includes extra bass hits to mirror the melodic shape of the riff and a hi-hat lift at the end to lead into beat one.

Example 4f

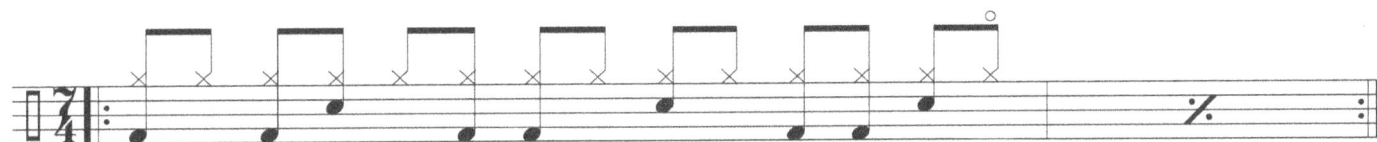

Now add these 1/16th note ghosts and a hi-hat lift before the last two snares to completely change the feel into a James Brown-style funk groove. Odd time signatures will work in almost any style if you use the appropriate sounds, articulation, embellishments and feel in the groove.

Example 4g

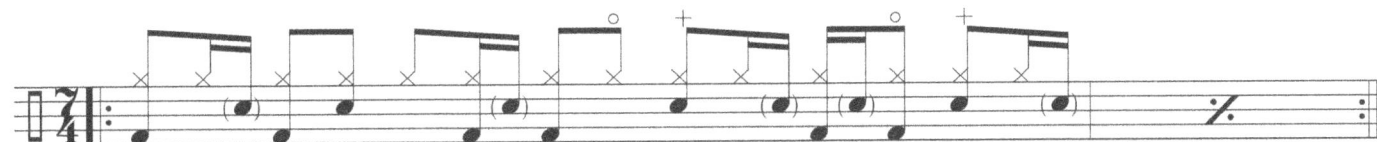

2+3+2 Odd Time Clave

Listen to track I and count "**1+2+1+2+3+1+2+**". This is a challenging odd time clave and doesn't often get played but is useful when combined with other odd time claves to create longer riffs.

Start with the basic ingredients to get the basic shape of the groove.

Example 4h

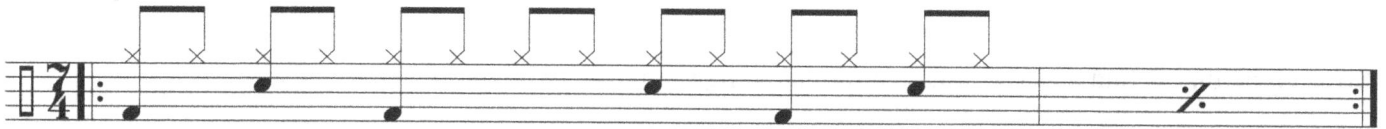

Now add 1/16th ghost notes and hi-hat lifts to make the groove funkier.

Example 4i

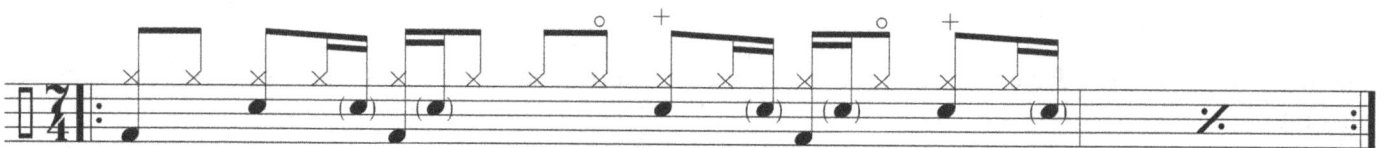

Combining 2+2+3 and 2+3+2 Odd Time Clave

This next example uses a combination of two different 7/4 claves to create a sophisticated four-bar groove. Listen to track J and count "**1+2+1+2+1+2+3+**" for the first three bars then "**1+2+1+2+3+1+2+**" for the fourth bar.

Example 4j

Use the following 1/16th ghost notes, hi-hat lifts and crashes to embellish the groove.

Example 4k

Now go back over these play-along tracks and experiment with your own variations on the grooves.

Chapter Five – 1/8th Note Fundamentals

The rest of the time signatures in this book have /8 (1/8th note divisions) as the bottom number, for example 5/8, 7/8 or 9/8.

Instead of counting a 1/4 note pulse as before, we now count the 1/8th note subdivisions in 2s and 3s. For example, we could count the five 1/8th notes in 5/8 as "**12123**" or "**12312**". There is no "and" between each count.

This combination of sets of two and three 1/8th note groups means the pulse length varies quickly in the bar and the music has a more irregular feel.

These are the basic ingredients we will combine to create odd time grooves before adding 1/16th notes later to create more variation and embellishments.

Groups of Two:

- Two 1/8th notes starting on the bass

- Two 1/8th notes starting on the snare

Groups of Three:

- Three 1/8th notes starting on the bass (nothing on 3)

- Three 1/8th notes starting on the bass (with snare on 3)

- Three 1/8th notes starting on the bass (with bass on 3)

- Three 1/8th notes starting on the snare (with nothing on 3)

- Three 1/8th notes starting on the snare (with snare on 3)

- Three 1/8th notes starting on the snare (with bass on 3)

These are all written out below.

Play around each one until you can comfortably feel the shape of the rhythm as you count either "12" or "123".

Two 1/8th notes starting on the bass drum.

Example 5a

Two 1/8th notes starting on the snare drum.

Example 5b

Three 1/8th notes starting on the bass drum.

Example 5c

Three 1/8th notes starting on the bass drum.

Example 5d

Three 1/8th notes starting on the bass drum.

Example 5e

Three 1/8th notes starting on the snare drum.

Example 5f

Three 1/8th notes starting on the snare drum.

Example 5g

Three 1/8th notes starting on the snare drum.

Example 5h

Chapter Six – 5/8

3+2 Odd Time Clave

Listen to track K and count "**12312**" through the eight-bar riff in 5/8. There are two pulses in each bar but the first beat is longer than the second beat because it lasts for three 1/8th notes while the second lasts for two. This is what gives the groove its "long-short, long-short" feeling.

The first chord lasts for four bars then ascends a tone for the second four bars.

Listen to the bass and keyboard playing on each pulse.

Let's combine the basic ingredients from examples 5c and 5b to build the shape of this groove.

Example 6a

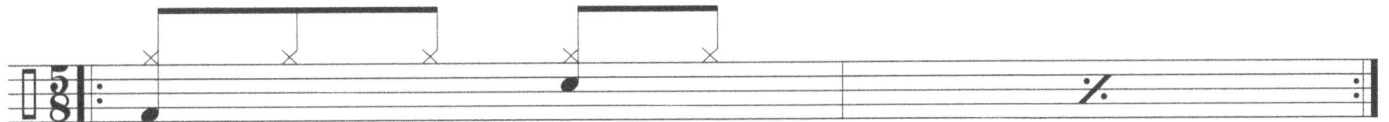

The following embellishments add a left hand 1/16th hi-hat which gives some energy, and a hi-hat lift on the second bar to draw attention to the back beat on the snare.

Example 6b

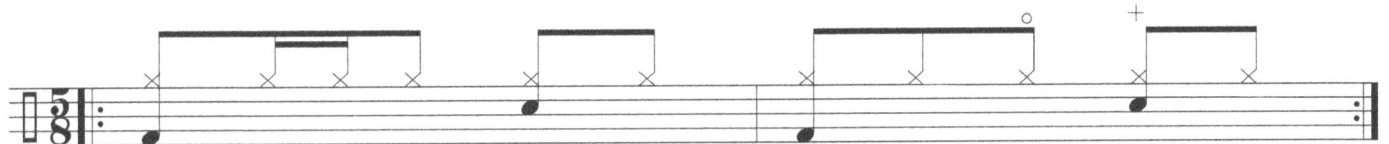

Adding the following bass drum hits helps to balance the groove and add more rhythmic interest.

Example 6c

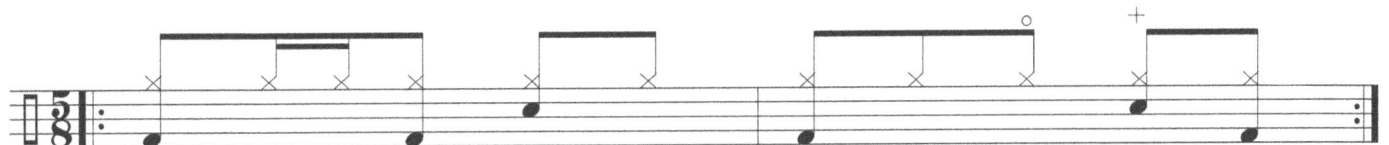

2+3 Odd Time Clave

Listen to track L and count "12123" throughout. In this eight-bar 5/8 riff the chords change every two bars. The bass plays on the first three 1/8th notes and the keyboard plays a chord on the second pulse in each bar to create a "short-long, short-long" feel.

Combine the basic ingredients of example 5a and example 5f to build the shape of this groove.

Notice how the 1/8th notes below are now beamed in groups of 2 + 3. I find it really helps when the beaming of the hi-hats matches the odd time clave of the groove. It's much clearer to see where the two beats sit in the bar.

Unfortunately, this isn't always the case with drum notation and I've often scribbled over parts to realign the beaming with the phrasing of the groove when sight reading at a gig.

Example 6d

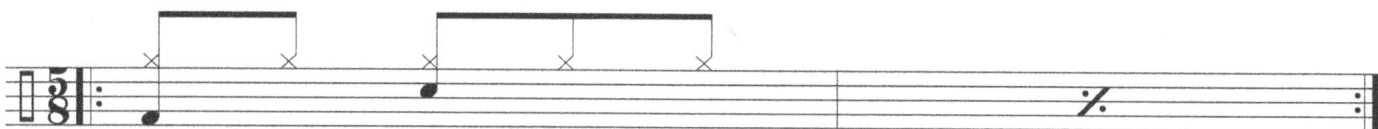

Add a bass drum on the second 1/8th note to mirror the bass part and a hi-hat lift at the end of the bar to emphasise the following downbeat.

Example 6e

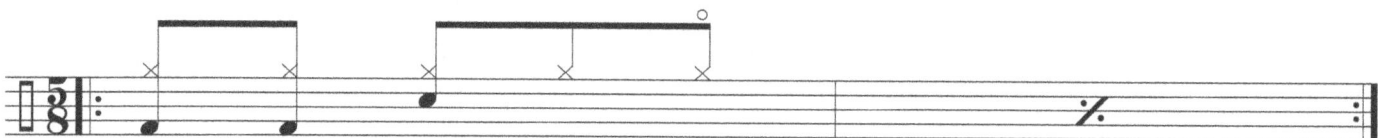

This last variation is busier and includes 1/16th hi-hat notes, and a two-over-three polyrhythmic subdivision on the snare drum on the second beat.

Example 6f

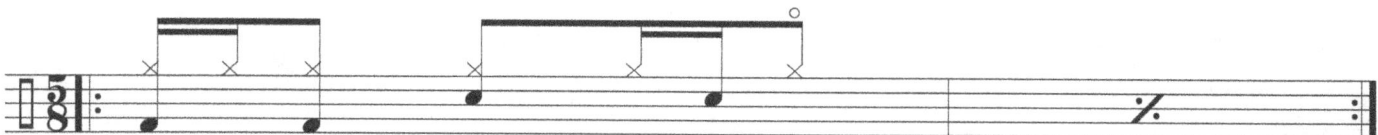

Combining 2+3 and 3+2 Odd Time Clave

This next example uses a combination of two different odd time claves in 5/8 to create a sophisticated four-bar groove. Listen to track M and count "**12123**" for the first three bars then "**12312**" for the fourth bar. Notice how the chords change on every bar and loop after four bars.

Start by combining the basic ingredients of example 5a and 5f for the first three bars, and then 5c and 5b to create the final bar.

Example 6g

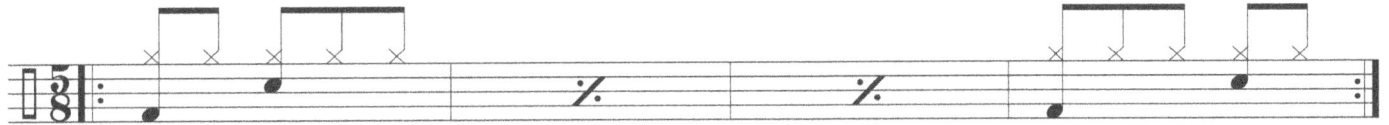

Add these bass drum hits to match the bass riff, and a hi-hat lift to emphasise the one.

Example 6h

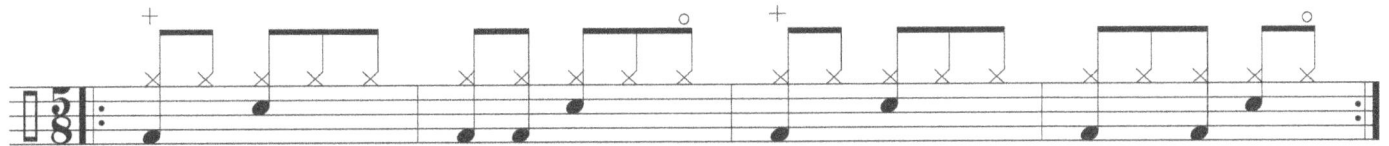

Finally, reintroduce some of the previous embellishments including the 1/16th hi-hat notes and two-over-three snare drum polyrhythm to create a more sophisticated groove.

Example 6i

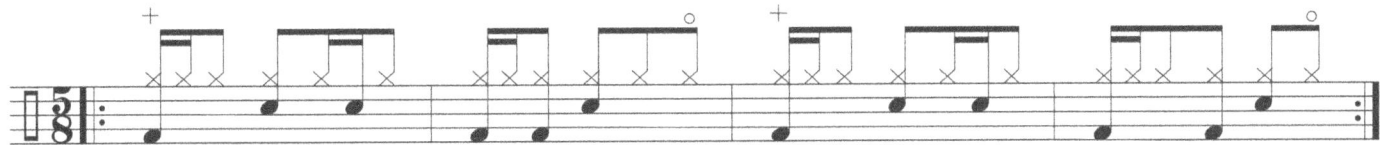

Chapter Seven – 7/8

2+2+3 Odd Time Clave

Listen to track N while counting "**1212123**". This six-bar riff in 7/8 time signature was inspired by the classic Dave Brubeck hit *Unsquare Dance*. Do check out the Spotify playlist if you aren't familiar with this tune. The chord sequence feels like a 12-bar blues because each bar of 7/8 sounds like two bars of a regular blues sequence in 4/4.

Here there are three pulse notes per bar. Before you add any embellishments or decorations, start by thinking about which snare and bass drum placements you'll use on each pulse and the shape they will create. Don't underestimate what a significant effect this can have on the feel of the music.

Let's start with what may seem the most obvious first choice: bass – snare – bass.

Example 7a

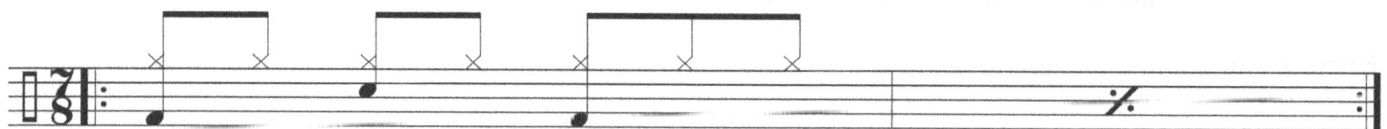

Now try playing bass – bass – snare. This shape creates more of a half-time feel, which dramatically changes the character of the music.

Example 7b

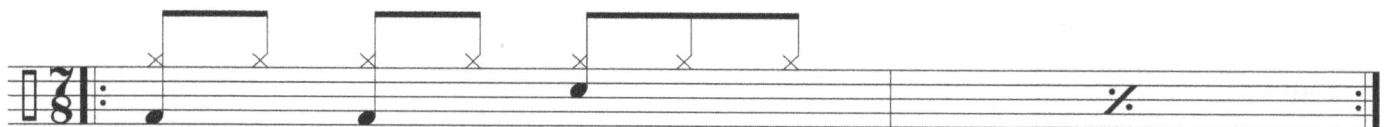

And finally try this bass – snare – snare variation which has more of a waltz feel.

Example 7c

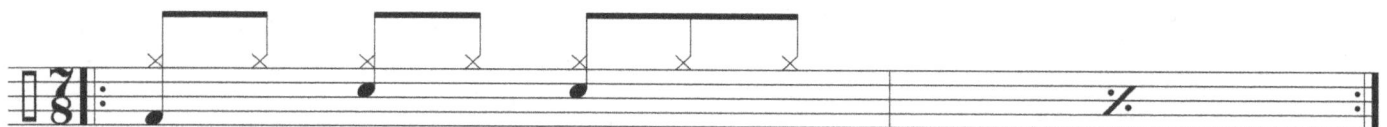

The take-away here is that by simply changing the bass and snare placements, the feel of the music is significantly altered – and that's before we think about adding any embellishments or decorations to the groove.

Add the following embellishments to Example 7a. The hi-hat lift helps to emphasise the down beat on one and the ghosted snare drum makes the groove a little funkier.

Example 7d

Now add these embellishments to Example 7b. Now, the hi-hat lift highlights the back beat on three and helps to emphasise the half time feel. The ghosted snare breaks up the triplet meter and the 1/16th note hi-hat notes at the beginning of the bar give the groove a busier feel.

Example 7e

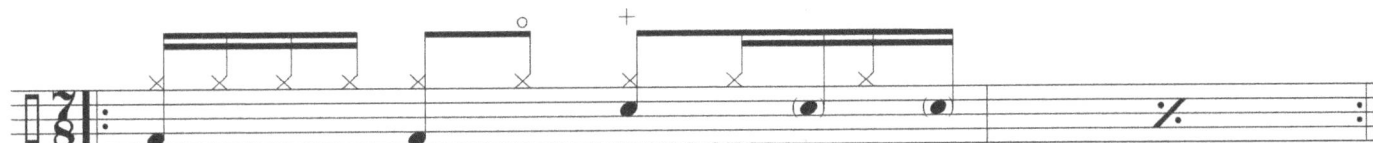

Now try these embellishments with Example 7c. The hi-hat lifts emphasise the snare drum on beats two and three, and the 1/16th notes add more interest to the end of the bar.

Example 7f

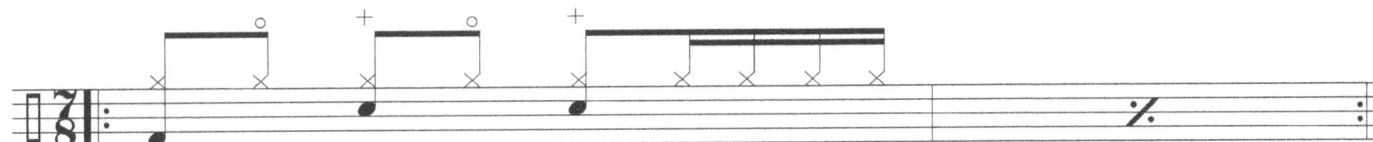

3+2+2 Odd Time Clave

Listen to track O and count "1231212" throughout. This twelve-bar blues in 7/8 is the division of 7/8 that I mentioned in the introduction to this book and is often heard in Slavic folk music.

The following example is my favourite beat to play on 7/8 and is Example 5d followed by 5a then 5b. I find that the extra snare on the end of the first triplet really helps to balance the groove.

Example 7g

Some of the Balkan folk music we played was pretty fast and I found that if I switched to the ride cymbal and used it to double the main snare and bass parts the groove could really swing. Listen to track P. At this faster tempo it seems like the groove takes on a completely different character and feels more like a 4/4 groove that has been stretched a bit!

Example 7h

Now return to the original tempo but with the following snare and bass drum placements on the last two beats. Again, how you orchestrate the bass and snare hits will really affect the character of the music. The next example combines the basic ingredients in examples 5c, 5b, 5a.

Example 7i

Now add these embellishments to create a two-bar phrase, which help make the groove funkier.

Example 7j

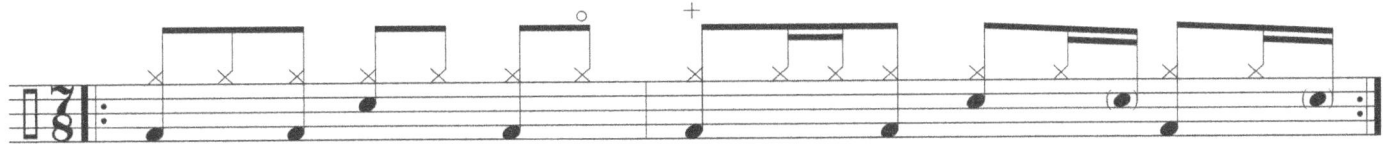

It's uncommon to place a snare on beat one, but doing so on the second bar of a loop can set up a half-time feel. This two-bar groove works nicely because the bass and snare alternate right across the bar line. This example combines the fundamental ingredients of examples 5c, 5b, 5a, 5f, 5a, and 5b.

Example 7k

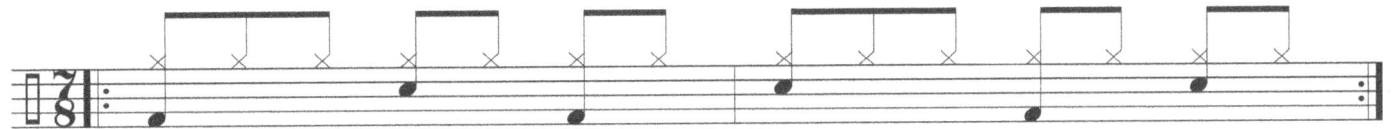

Adding the hi-hat lift before the snare at the beginning of the second bar really highlights the half-time feel. The extra bass notes now closely mirror the bassline and the ghost notes on the snare make this groove a lot funkier.

Example 7l

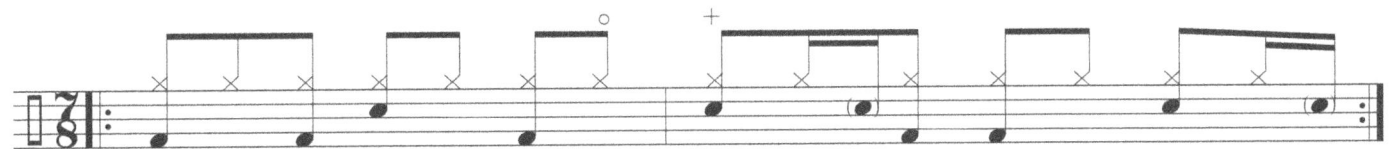

2+3+2 Odd Time Clave

This 7/8 odd time clave isn't often used as a one-bar loop but can work well as part of a longer phrase combining other clave variations. So while this example isn't common, it is important to be comfortable with any division of the bar. Listen to track Q and count "1212312" through this eight-bar chord sequence.

Adding the extra bass note at the end of the 3s in beat two helps to balance out the groove, as you did in Example 7g.

Example 7m

These simple hi-hat embellishments at the end of each measure help to highlight beat one and keep your place in the loop.

Example 7n

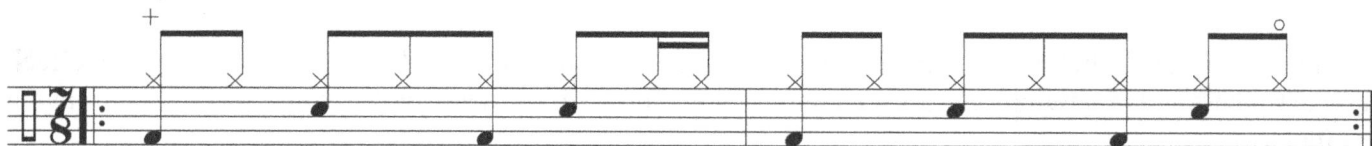

Combining 2+2+3 and 2+3+2 Odd Time Clave

This next example uses two different odd time claves to create a sophisticated four-bar groove in 7/8. Listen to track R and count "1212123" for the first three bars then "1212312" for the fourth. Notice how the chords change on every bar and loop after four bars.

Start by combining basic ingredients to build the basic shape of the groove.

Example 7o

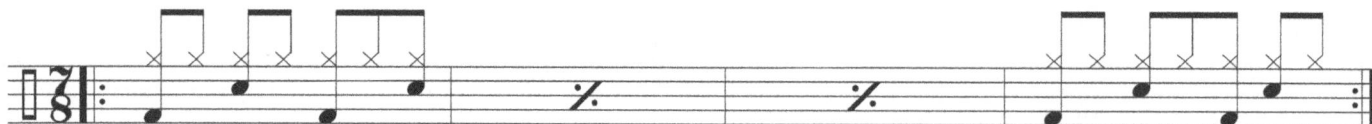

Now use these embellishments and extra bass hits to further shape the groove and add some interest.

Example 7p

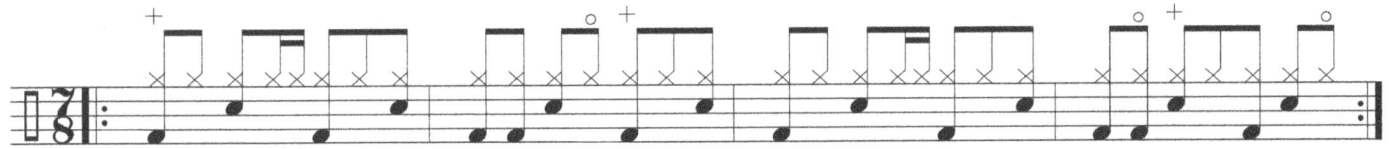

After some practice playing along with the track you will learn the sound of the riff and no longer need to keep counting in twos and threes. When you reach this point, experiment with your own combinations and ideas using all the basic ingredients.

Try to add some variations while you play, but don't lose the fundamental shape of the groove!

Chapter Eight – 9/8

The most common version of 9/8 that you will come across is 3+3+3, which is really just 3/4 with a triplet meter. Personally, I don't think of that as an odd time groove because it is all threes. However, using a combination of twos and threes can create some interesting rhythmic phrases which feel more like odd time grooves.

(2+2) + (2+3) Odd Time Clave

Listen carefully to track S and you'll hear there is a chord change on the fifth quaver. Thinking 4+5, while counting "121212123", makes sense because it is in sync with the harmonic structure of the music.

Start by combining the fundamental ingredients to build the basic shape of the groove.

Example 8a

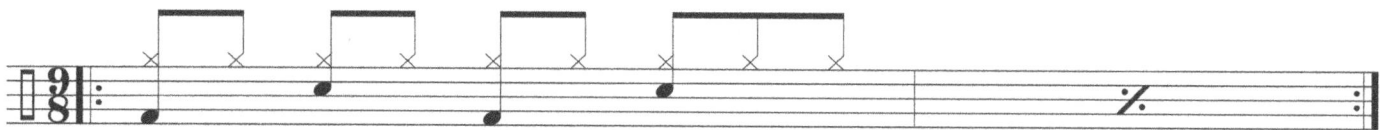

Now add these embellishments to shape the phrase and create a two-bar groove to match the two-bar chord sequence.

Example 8b

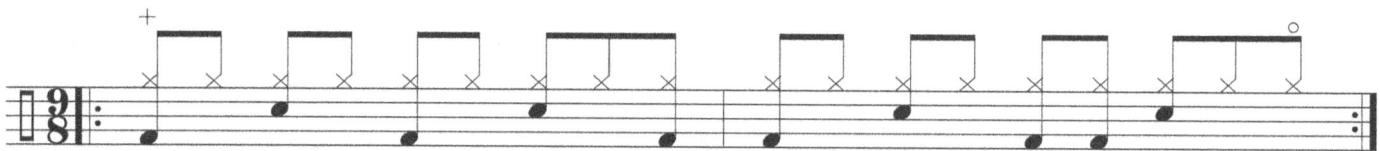

(3+2) + (2+2) Odd Time Clave

Listen to track T. It has a bit of a Cuban montuno feel to it, but don't worry about having to play any complicated cow bell patterns in odd times! It works fine just keeping to the basic 1/8th notes on hi-hat, snare and bass drum. Listen to the track and you'll hear that the shape of the riff is 5+4 because of where the chords change in this two-bar riff.

Count "123121212" and play the basic ingredients to get the essential shape of the groove.

Example 8c

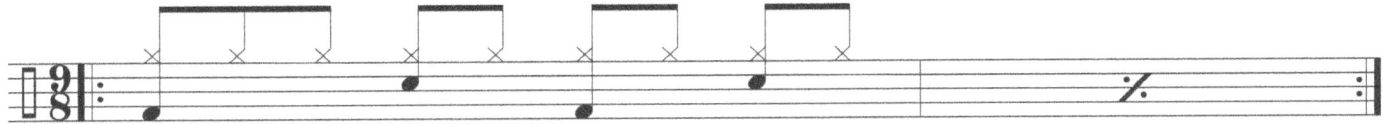

Adding some toms helps to create more of a mambo feel and generates a two-bar pattern to match the two-bar chord sequence.

Example 8d

(2+3) + (2+2) Odd Time Clave

Listen to track U. Like the previous example, you can think of this groove as 5+4. Hear the chord change on the sixth quaver. However, the first half of the bar is now a 2+3 clave, which totally changes the feel of the groove.

Count "121231212" when playing the basic ingredients of this groove.

Example 8e

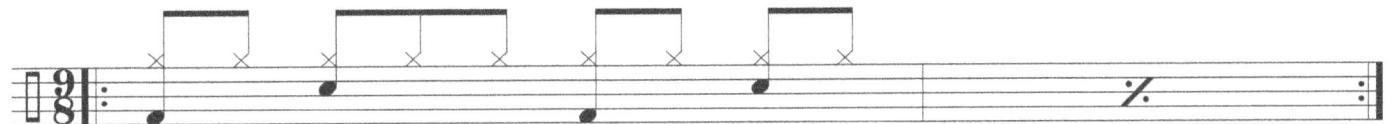

Now add the following embellishments to make the phrase a little groovier.

Example 8f

Combining 2+2+2+3 and 2+3+2+2 Odd Time Clave

Listen to track V. Combining different clave patterns is an effective way to create complex sounding grooves. Having established the odd time clave in the first three bars, this four-bar riff changes up in the last bar and throws your sense of pulse to add tension to the music.

Example 8g

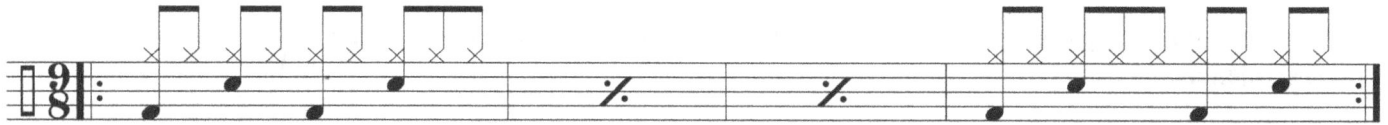

Now embellish the groove with some extra bass hits, hi-hat lifts and 1/16th ghost notes to add more levels to the phrase.

Example 8h

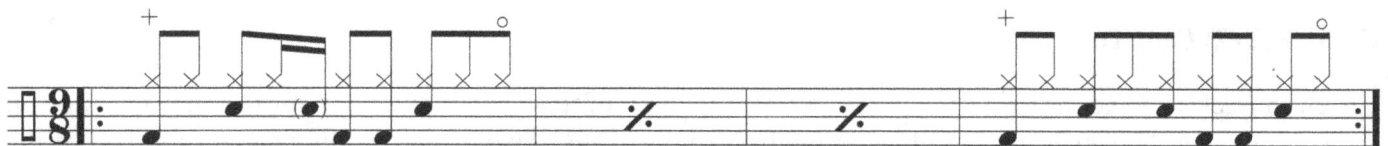

When you're feeling confident, go back and play with the tracks again, but this time experiment with your own embellishments, variations and ideas.

Just make sure you stick to the correct clave and focus on locking in with the other instruments.

Chapter Nine – 11/8

It's useful to think of longer time signatures as two bars of different time signatures added together to create more manageable sections. When I do this, I imagine an invisible bar line that separates the longer bar into two shorter ones and the first task is to figure out exactly where the hidden bar line should go.

It's common to divide a bar of 11/8 into 6+5 or 5+6, but it could be 7+4 or any other combination. Listening out for chord changes within the bar will be helpful in figuring out the phrasing of the division.

Then I find where the twos and threes are within those two halves of the bar and correct the beaming on the notation to match.

While 9/8 odd time grooves are mainly divided into twos with one group of three, 11/8 is normally divided into groups of three with one group of two to disrupt the pattern.

There are many possible odd time clave variations in 11/8. The following examples are just a few common ideas to get you started, but of course you can explore this subject as extensively as you wish.

6+5 = (3+3) + (2+3) Odd Time Clave

Audio track W is a two-bar riff with a descending bassline. There is a chord change on the seventh quaver of each bar which creates a 6+5 feel to the phrase.

Start with the following 1/8th note fundamentals to build the basic shape of the groove.

Example 9a

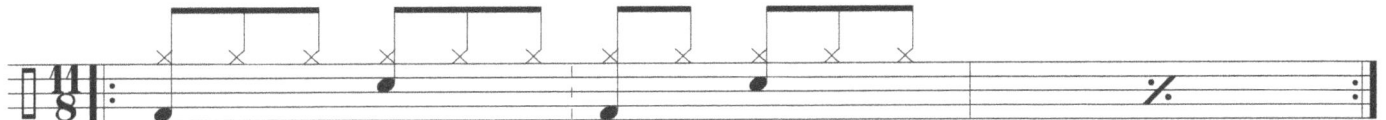

Now add some extra bass drum hits to embellish the shape, and hi-hat lifts to highlight the subdivision.

Example 9b

5+6 = (3+2) + (3+3) Odd Time Clave

Listen to audio track X. This two-bar riff has a chord change on the sixth quaver of each bar which gives the 5+6 feel to the music. Start by mapping out the 1/8th note groupings to get the basic shape of the groove.

Example 9c

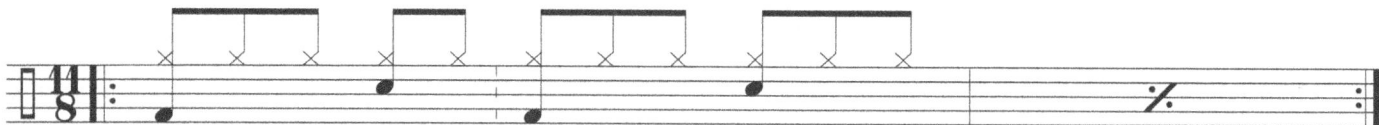

Again, added hi-hat lifts help to clarify the hidden bar line that splits the bar in two. An extra bass drum reinforces the triplet shuffle feel.

Example 9d

7+4 = (2+2+3) + (2+2) Odd Time Clave

The odd time clave in track Y is primarily built from twos with a three to disrupt the pattern. This two-bar riff has a chord change on the 1/8th quaver of each bar which creates the 7+4 feel. Start by mapping the 1/8th note groupings below to create the shape of the groove.

Example 9e

Now add some embellishments. Notice how the 1/16th notes in the second bar add energy. Experiment with some of your own variations using these ingredients across both bars.

Example 9f

Return to the 1/8th note fundamentals and change the bass and snare drum placements as you did in Chapter Seven. By placing the snare drum on beat eight we give the same piece of music a half time feel, which can be used to create contrast between different sections of a tune. You could use the half time feel on the verse and the regular feel on the chorus to lift the energy.

Example 9g

Now add embellishments to this basic shape. 1/16th hi-hat notes are a good way to change the feel without altering the shape of the beat.

Example 9h

Chapter Ten – 13/8

We can create 13/8 grooves using the same method as in the previous chapter. First of all, listen for a natural split in the bar to find the primary subdivision, for example 8+5, 9+4, or 7+6, then find the twos and threes within those.

Again, there are many possible division variations in 13/8 and the following examples are just a few common ideas to get you going. I recommend you listen to drummers who use a lot of odd times and try copying the divisions that you like to take this concept further.

8+5 = (2+2+2+2) + (3+2)

In track Z the two-bar riff has a chord change on the ninth quaver of each bar which gives the music an 8+5 subdivision, and this is where the dotted line is placed on the notation. However, you can think of the eight 1/8th notes as a 4/4 bar and view the entire thing as 4/4 + 5/8. This has four pulse notes in the first half (4/4) and two pulse notes in the second half (5/8).

Example 10a

When you're comfortable with this shape, experiment by adding embellishments to the groove. Adding some ghosted snares makes this variation funkier and the hi-hat lift helps to mark the invisible bar line and the end of the complete phrase.

The notation can make examples like this look pretty daunting. But music written down always *looks* harder than it is! Just break it down into sections and work on them separately (use the dotted bar line to help with this), then join them back together. Remember that the 1/8th notes are always beamed in 2s and 3s to outline the subdivisions.

Example 10b

9+4 = (3+3+3) + (2+2)

In audio track AA, the riff contains a chord change on the tenth quaver of each bar giving the music a 9+4 subdivision which is where the dotted line is placed on the notation. You could think of this groove as 9/8 + 2/4, with three triplet meter pulse notes in the first half and two duple meter pulse notes in the second half.

Be careful with the placement of the final note of the third triplet, which somehow feels a little late.

Example 10c

This time, these familiar embellishments create a more syncopated two-bar groove. When you're ready, experiment with some of your own as you play along with the track.

Example 10d

7+6 = (2+2+3) + (3+3)

Listen to track BB. The chord change on the 8th quaver gives this music a 7+6 subdivision, rather than a 4+9 feel which we could be tempted to count if we were only thinking of the drums. The dotted bar line helps to clarify where this subdivision is in the bar.

Example 10e

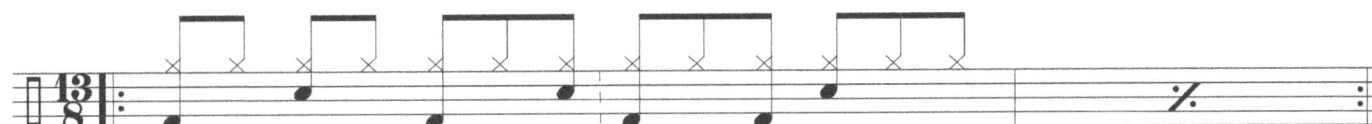

Now embellish the shape with familiar elements to add more interest. The hi-hat lift helps to highlight the end of each bar, the ghosted snare adds some funk, and the extra bass lengthens the groove into a two-bar phrase.

Example 10f

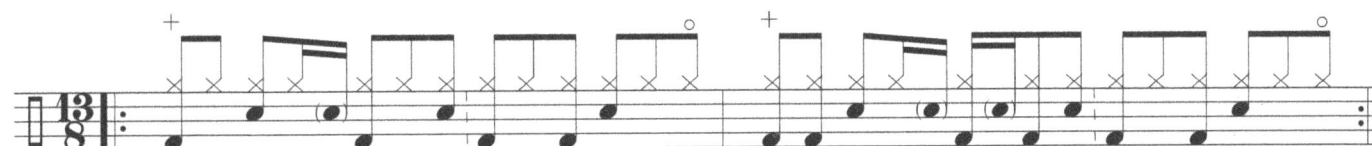

5+8 = (2+3) + (2+2+2+2)

In audio track CC the two-bar riff has a chord change on the sixth quaver of each bar creating a 5+8 subdivision. This is not the same as simply reversing the first 13/8 example (8+5) because of the way the harmony resolves. The groove feels quite different when played with this chord sequence.

The more fluent you become with this material, the easier it will be for you select a groove most suitable to the shape of the music.

If you think of the final eight quavers as a regular 4/4 bar then what you really have here is a 5/8 + 4/4 groove with two pulse notes in the first half (5/8) and four pulse notes in the second half (4/4).

Example 10g

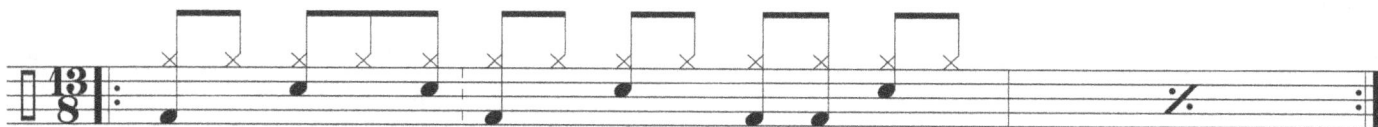

Now embellish the shape with hi-hat lifts and 1/16th note ghosts to create interest. The different bass drum pattern in the second bar creates a two-bar groove.

Example 10h

42

Chapter Eleven – Basic Fills

When playing odd time fills it is important to know the number of beats they cover and what their meter is. As with grooves, they're all about thinking in groups of twos and threes, so you need to be sure of the length of each beat you are filling over – either two or three 1/4 notes or two or three 1/8th notes.

The following examples provide some basic rhythmic ideas on the snare drum, but you should also practice playing them around the kit using the toms. See how many different fills you can create from each rhythmic idea. Try to develop a solid library of basic fills that fit over different subdivisions which you can embellish later to suit more specific grooves.

One Beat Fills – Duple Meter (Twos)

These fills will feel familiar from playing in 4/4 time.

Play each one after hearing the clicks on the first three beats and land on the crash at the beginning of the second bar.

Example 11a

One Beat Fills – Triple Meter (Threes)

These fills will feel familiar from playing in 12/8 time.

Play each fill after hearing the clicks on the first three beats and land on the crash.

Example 11b

Applying basic fills to odd time grooves

The following examples offer a few combinations of different fills with different odd time grooves. It helps to work through them systematically, clarifying the number of beats and meter of each fill.

After you can play each exercise comfortably you should make up your own variations for each fill while jamming along with the audio tracks.

One Beat Fills – Duple Meter (Twos)

These fills can be used in any /4 time signature and any /8 time signature if it has a two at the end of the riff.

Listen again to audio track A. This example combines Example 3b with duple meter fill two.

Remember, when you are playing a /4 time signature, every beat is in duple meter. The threes and twos come from the groupings of the main pulse notes, which are divided as "**1**+2+3+**1**+2+" in this 5/4 groove.

Example 11c

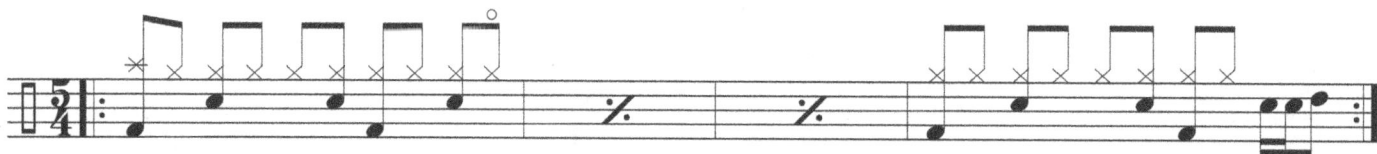

Listen again to track G. The next example combines Example 4c with duple meter fill three. This groove has a 2+2+3 clave in 7/4 and is counted "**1**+2+**1**+2+**1**+2+3+".

Example 11d

Listen again to track K. This example combines Example 6c with duple meter fill four. This groove is in 5/8 with a 3+2 odd time clave, so count "**12312**" throughout.

Example 11e

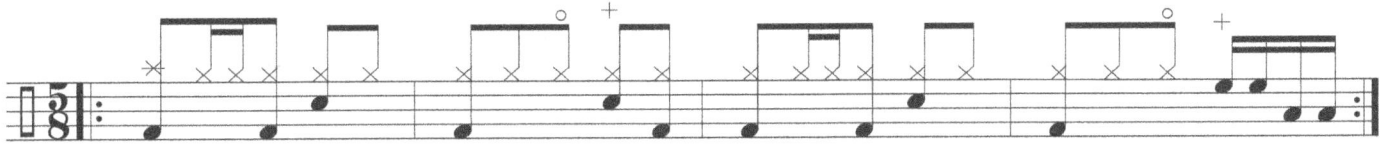

One Beat Fills – Triple Meter (Threes)

These fills don't work in /4 time signatures, but they do work in /8 time signatures if they have a three at the end of the bar.

Listen again to track L. This 5/8 example combines Example 6f with triple meter fill two and is counted "**12123**".

Example 11f

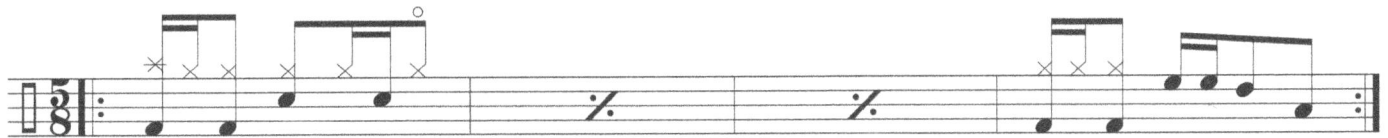

Listen again to track N. This 7/8 groove is counted "**1212123**" and combines Example 7d with triple meter fill three.

Example 11g

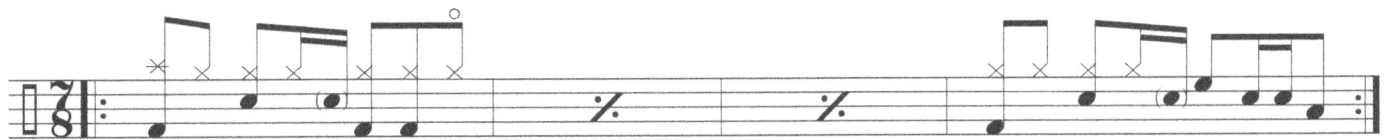

Listen again to track S. This 9/8 groove is counted "**121212123**" and combines Example 8b with triple meter fill four.

Example 11h

Two Beat Fills – Duple Meter (Twos)

These fills can be used in any /4 time signature and some /8 time signatures if they have two 2s at the end of the riff.

Listen again to track B. This 5/4 groove is counted "**1**+2+**1**+2+3+" and combines Example 3f with duple meter fills two and three.

Example 11i

Listen again to track O. This 7/8 groove is counted "**1231212**" and combines Example 7j with duple meter fills four and five.

Example 11j

Listen again to track AA. This 13/8 groove is counted "**1231231231212**". It combines Example 10d with duple meter fills one and two.

Example 11k

Two Beat Fills – Triple Meter (Threes)

These fills don't work in /4 time signatures but they do work in some /8 time signatures if they have two 3s at the end of the riff.

Listen again to track X. This 11/8 groove is counted "**12312123123**". It combines Example 9d with triple meter fills five and six.

Example 11l

Listen again to track BB. This 13/8 groove is counted "**1212123123123**" and combines Example 10f with triple meter fills seven and eight.

Example 11m

Two Beat Fills – Mixed Meter (Twos and Threes)

These fills don't work in /4 time signatures, but they do work in some /8 time signatures when they have a group of three and a two at the end of the riff. Just make sure you know which way around they go!

Listen again to track W. It combines Example 9b with duple meter fill 2 and triple meter fill 2. The 11/8 groove is counted "**12312312123**".

Example 11n

The 13/8 groove in audio track Z is counted "1212121212312". It combines Example 10b with triple meter fill three and duple meter fill four.

Example 11o

Finally, let's add a pick-up to each different fill to help blur the edges. When doing this I still think of the fills as just one or two beats long, but they simply have a pick-up added. I find this much easier than thinking of them as entirely new rhythms.

Listen again to track D. This final example combines Example 3j with duple meter fill five which is given a pick-up. This 5/4 groove is counted "**1**e+a 2e+a 3e+a **1**e+a 2e+a".

Example 11p

Chapter Twelve - Polyrhythmic Fills

Polyrhythmic fills can be used to create tension by making it seem like you are *stretching* the time with your fills. They can also displace beat one for the listener (a common effect in contemporary music) and are particularly effective when combined with odd time grooves. It's quite a simple concept, but it is not easy to accurately place the notes.

Polyrhythms superimpose a new beat subdivision over the top of the main subdivision and are written with a number over the top of the notes that shows this temporary new subdivision for that beat.

These are the three most common polyrhythmic fills.

Two over Three

When playing in triple meter you can use a two-over-three subdivision to create a polyrhythmic fill. In this example the two 1/8th notes are evenly spaced across the final triple meter beat.

Start by playing the fill on the snare drum with a regular 12/8 beat.

Example 12a

Listen again to track L. The next example uses this fill around the toms with Example 6e, a 5/8 groove with a 2+3 clave.

Example 12b

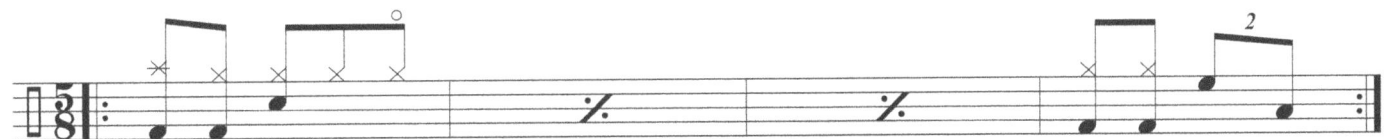

Three-Over-Two

In duple meter you can use a three-over-two subdivision to create a polyrhythmic fill. In this example the three 1/8th notes are evenly spaced across the duration of the final duple meter beat.

Start by playing the fill on the snare with a regular 4/4 beat.

Example 12c

Listen to track O. It is a 7/8 groove with a 3+2+2 odd time clave.

This example shows the fill played around the toms with Example 7g,

Example 12d

Four-Over-Three

When playing in a triple meter you can use a four-over-three subdivision to create a polyrhythmic fill.

In this example, the four 1/16th notes are evenly spaced across the last triple meter beat.

Start by playing the fill on the snare drum with a regular 12/8 beat.

Example 12e

Listen again to track X, an 11/8 groove with a 3+2+3+3 clave. The next example shows the four-over-three fill applied around the toms with Example 9d.

Example 12f

Combining Polyrhythmic Fills

Combining different polyrhythmic fills increases the effect of stretching the time during your fills, which is a great way to create tension and excitement, and is where things get very interesting!

Before attempting to play the notated examples, listen to the audio track several times until you have the sound of the polyrhythmic combinations clear in your mind. Take your time with each exercise to make sure you are accurately placing every note.

Listen again to track K, which is a simple 5/8 groove with a 3+2 clave using Example 6a.

Start by playing this fill on the snare drum.

Example 12g

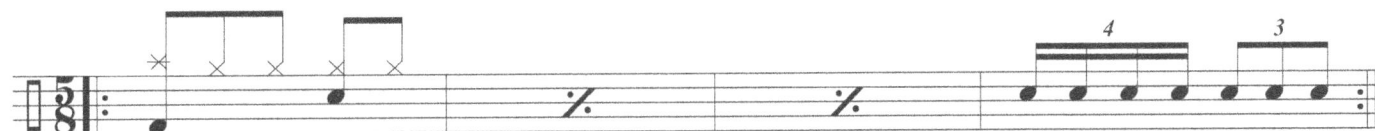

Now play the fill around the toms to help blur the second pulse note and create what feels like seven stretched over five.

Example 12h

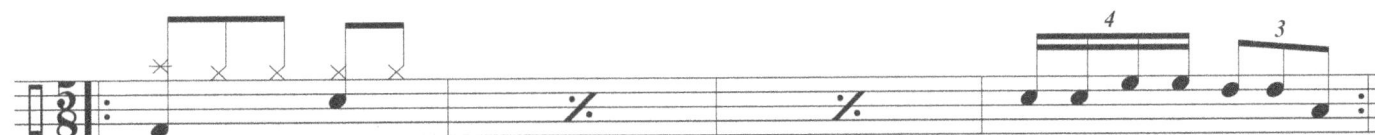

Listen again to track N, a basic 7/8 groove with a 2+2+3 odd time clave built around Example 7b. The next example uses the same polyrhythmic fills in reverse.

Example 12i

Finally, mixing basic fills with polyrhythmic fills can create some very interesting rhythmic phrases with almost infinite variety.

Listen again to track Y.

The next example adds a mix of basic and polyrhythmic fills to Example 9g, which is an 11/8 groove with a 2+2+3, 2+2 odd time clave. Remember, polyrhythms have numbers written over each beat. If there is no number, then it is a regular fill.

Example 12j

Chapter Thirteen – Combining Odd Time Signatures

So far, you have explored many time signatures and combined different odd time claves to create interesting grooves. However, you have only dealt with one time signature at a time.

This chapter offers a few examples of how you can combine different time signatures to build more complex phrasing over longer loops.

The variations and combinations available are virtually limitless, so I'm just going to offer a few samples to demonstrate an idea, along with some tracks to practice along to. You can apply this process to any combination of any time signatures, in any style of music. As I said at the very beginning, it's all just twos and threes!

Before attempting to play any of the following examples, take a moment to make sure you are clear about the odd time clave in each different bar. The beaming of the notes will give you a good clue in these examples, but you can't always rely on that to be correct when reading drum charts on a gig. Always listen to the riff and make sure you know where the twos and threes are before you start playing.

Listen to track DD.

This first example is three bars of 5/4 (3+2) then one bar of 5/8 (3+2), which makes the last bar feel like the time has sped up and that the repeat comes in early.

Start by getting comfortable with the basic 1/8th note groove with a hi-hat lift at the end that marks the loop point.

Example 13a

Now add some ghost 1/16th note embellishments and extra hi-hat lifts to mark the end of each bar. This example uses a duple meter fill on the last beat with a pick up note on the high tom. Once you can comfortably play this version, experiment with different duple meter fills from Chapter Eleven.

Example 13b

Listen to track EE.

This example is three bars of 7/4 (3+2+2) followed by two bars of 7/8 (2+2+3). Again, start by getting comfortable with the basic shape of the groove.

Example 13c

Sometimes, a very small embellishment, or even just re-orchestrating a couple of notes, can completely change the feel of the groove. This example adds a hi-hat lift before the first snare, which makes it feel funkier, and the last two snares are re-orchestrated to the high tom.

The fill on the final beat is triple meter, so experiment with different fills from Example 11b.

Example 13d

Listen to track FF.

Example 13e uses three different time signatures over a four-bar loop. The groove is 9/8 (3+2+2+2), 7/8 (3+2+2), 9/8 (3+2+2+2, 11/8 (3+3+2+3).

Again, start by playing the basic ingredients until you are completely comfortable with the shape of the groove.

Watch out for the two bass hits at the end of the 7/8 bar!

Example 13e

Now add some 1/16th ghost note embellishments and a fill at the end of the loop. Again, the last beat is triple meter so experiment with the different fills from Example 11b.

Example 13f

Listen to track GG which uses three different time signatures over a four-bar loop.

The groove is 13/8 (3+3+3+2+2), 5/8 (3+2), 13/8 (3+3+3+2+2), 7/8 (2+2+3).

Again, start by playing the basic ingredients until you are comfortable with the shape of the groove.

Example 13g

Now add some embellishments and a fill at the end of the loop. The last beat is triple meter, so try some variations of the 2 over 3 polyrhythmic fills.

Example 13h

Listen to track HH. This final example uses four different time signatures over a four-bar loop, with each bar being an 1/8th note longer than the previous bar.

The chords change on each bar and feature a common pop chord sequence which I thought would be fun to mess with over this groove.

The groove is 5/8 (3+2), 7/8 (3+2+2), 9/8 (3+2+2+2), 11/8 (3+2+3+3).

Practice the basic ingredients until you are confident with the shape of the groove.

Example 13i

Now add some embellishments and a fill at the end of the loop.

There's a lot going on in this groove, so make sure you are comfortable with all the details. The fill is played over the last two beats, both of which are triple meter, but the final beat uses a 4 over 3 polyrhythm.

Experiment with different orchestrations of the fill to create new variations on the same idea.

Example 13j

All Remaining Time Signatures

For the purposes of this book I have focused on time signatures that require you to count with a *combination* of groups of two and three.

If you can count a time signature using *only* twos or *only* threes then it's not an odd time signature, and these are called simple or compound time signatures.

For example, while 3 may be an odd number, 3/4 is not an odd time signature because it is counted in *only* groups of two (**1**+2+3+). Likewise, 6/4 can be counted **1**+2+3+**1**+2+3+ *or* **1**+2+**1**+2+**1**+2+ I.e., either twos or threes but *not both*. The same is true of 3/8 (**123**) and 6/8 (**123,123** or **12,12,12**).

I have omitted some odd time signatures because they are very rarely used. They are so long as to be impractical and are usually notated as combinations of shorter time signatures.

For example, 9/4 is rarely seen because it is clearer to notate the music as a bar of 5/4 followed by a bar of 4/4, or the other way around depending on the shape of the groove.

Which would you prefer to sight read?

Likewise, 11/4 can be more conveniently notated as 6/4 + 5/4, or 4/4 + 4/4 + 3/4, or whatever combination makes most sense with the music. Trust me, no one wants to read a bar of 11/4! The same applies to 15/8 and 17/8, which is why I've also left those out.

12/8 is nearly always grouped as four even triplets, but it is possible to combine twos and threes, like in the classic West Side Story tune "America". However, when this happens it is usually notated as 6/8 + 3/4 as it more clearly represents the shape of the music.

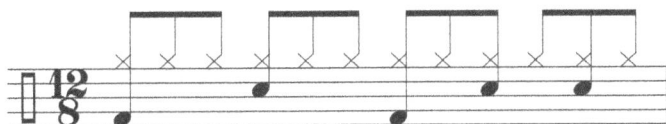

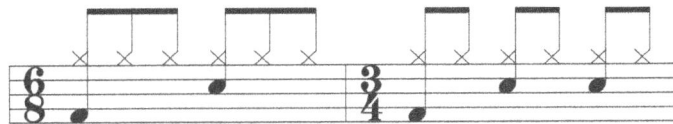

Conclusion

This book has covered the essential concepts and techniques required for playing odd time grooves. I hope you enjoyed developing these skills, and that your knowledge and confidence has increased to the point where you feel comfortable playing with other musicians and creating your own music. Playing with other musicians should always be the goal.

Learning to play music is a lifelong pursuit – it takes work but is extremely rewarding. The more you practice, the more you improve. The more you study, the more you will understand and appreciate this great art form and get the most pleasure out of your journey.

You can reach me through my website **www.busterbirch.co.uk** where you can join my mailing list to receive free practice resources and updates on future publications.

Best wishes and thank you.

Buster

P.S. If you've enjoyed this book, please do leave a review on Amazon – it really helps to spread the word about what we do.

Appendix

Clarification of Musical Terms and Definitions

Some of the terms used to describe music can be confusing because they can mean different things in different contexts. In the interest of clarification, I would like to take a moment to explain a few musical terms that are referenced in this book.

Theory vs Use

Drum notation has yet to be standardised. The same rhythm can often be notated in more than one way, so you have to make a choice. In this situation, I find that a good guideline is, *the less ink on the page, the better.*

Tempo vs Subdivision

Tempo has an effect on how we notate music. The level of subdivision we choose to represent the notes is determined by the tempo and how we count it. Usually, the faster the music, the smaller the note value. We tend to use 5/8 notation if we count the five quickly and 5/4 notation if we count the five slowly. Either can be used for both, but this protocol makes a lot of sense.

Meter

The meter is the subdivision of each pulse and is referred to as either *duple meter* (subdivisions of two) or *triple meter* (subdivisions of three).

Pulse

Pulse is subjective and depends on how the music is notated and counted… this can get a little bit confusing!

Essentially, the pulse is how we count and feel the music and is often seen as how many *beats* there are in a bar. This comes from classical music, where the conductor waves the baton to mark each pulse.

This is true when working in time signatures with a /4 underneath as the pulse is equal to the number of beats in the bar. 5/4 has a pulse of five in each bar. However, there are strong and weak pulses which affect the feel of the music and these are grouped in groups of two or three 1/4 notes that are evenly split into 1/8th notes.

When working in time signatures with an /8 underneath the pulse is subject to the meter. 5/8 has two pulses in each bar which are subdivided in to triple meter (groups of three) and duple meter (groups of two)

For example, 5/8 could be divided as a group of two 1/8th notes followed by a group of three 1/8th notes, or three 1/8th notes followed by two 1/8th notes. Either way, there are two pulses in each bar, but the length of each beat would be different.

Simple Time Signatures

Simple time signatures *only* use duple meter (2/4, 3/4, 4/4, 5/4, 6/4, 7/4, 9/4, 11/4). The pulse is regular and equal to the top number for each time signature. E.g., 3/4 has a pulse of three (three 1/4 note beats per bar) and each pulse is subdivided into two (duple meter).

Compound Time Signatures

Compound time signatures *only* use triple meter (6/8, 9/8, 12/8, 15/8). The pulse is regular (even) but you subdivide the top number of each time signature by three to find the number of the pulses in the bar. For example, 6/8 has a pulse of two (two beats per bar) and each pulse is subdivided into groups of three (triple meter).

Mixed Meter Time Signatures

These odd time signatures use a mixture of duple and triple meter and have an irregular pulse (5/8, 7/8, 11/8, 13/8). When dealing with mixed meter it is important to be aware of the sequence of groupings of the meter – what I refer to as the *odd time clave*.

5/8 has only two beats per bar (one duple meter and one triple meter) but the sequence could be 3+2 or 2+3. 7/8 has three beats per bar (two duple meter and one triple meter) but the sequence could be 2+2+3, 2+3+2, or 3+2+2.

Using a different sequence of meter groupings has a significant effect on how the music feels because it doesn't just affect the rhythm but also the harmonic and melodic phrasing of the piece.

Play-along Audio Tracks (Minus Drums)

Track A: 5/4 (3+2)

Track B: 5/4 (2+3)

Track C: 5/4 (3+2, 3+2, 3+2, 2+3)

Track D: 5/4 (3+2)

Track E: 5/4 (2+3)

Track F: 5/4 (2+3, 3+2)

Track G: 7/4 (2+2+3)

Track H: 7/4 (3+2+2)

Track I: 7/4 (2+3+2)

Track J: 7/4 (2+2+3, 2+2+3, 2+2+3, 2+3+2)

Track K: 5/8 (3+2)

Track L: 5/8 (2+3)

Track M: 5/8 (2+3, 2+3, 2+3, 3+2)

Track N: 7/8 (2+2+3)

Track O: 7/8 (3+2+2)

Track P: 7/8 (3+2+2)

Track Q: 7/8 (2+3+2)

Track R: 7/8 (2+2+3, 2+2+3, 2+2+3, 2+3+2)

Track S: 9/8 (2+2+2+3)

Track T: 9/8 (3+2+2+2)

Track U: 9/8 (2+3+2+2)

Track V: 9/8 (2+2+2+3, 2+2+2+3, 2+2+2+3, 2+3+2+2)

Track W: 11/8 (3+3+2+3)

Track X: 11/8 (3+2+3+3)

Track Y: 11/8 (2+2+3+2+2)

Track Z: 13/8 (2+2+2+2+3+2)

Track AA: 13/8 (3+3+3+2+2)

Track BB: 13/8 (2+2+3+3+3)

Track CC: 13/8 (2+3+2+2+2+2)

Track DD: 5/4 (3+2), 5/4 (3+2), 5/4 (3+2), 5/8 (3+2)

Track EE: 7/4 (3+2+2), 7/4 (3+2+2), 7/4 (3+2+2), 7/8 (2+2+3), 7/8 (2+2+3)

Track FF: 9/8 (3+2+2+2), 7/8 (3+2+2), 9/8 (3+2+2+2, 11/8 (3+3+2+3)

Track GG: 13/8 (3+3+3+2+2), 5/8 (3+2), 13/8 (3+3+3+2+2), 7/8 (2+2+3)

Track HH: 5/8 (3+2), 7/8 (3+2+2), 9/8 (3+2+2+2), 11/8 (3+2+3+3)